STATE OF HAWAII · CITY AND COUNTY OF HONOLULU

HONOLULU

THEN & NOW

By ROLAND MORGAN

Bodima Books

W9-DEX-271

Copyright © Roland Morgan 1978

ISBN-0-88875 - 003-X

Cover design by Roland Morgan and Bob Masse; artwork by Bob Masse

This book is for Dilys and Tudor

Honolulu's
Hawaiian Directions

Mauka
(towards the mountains)
Ewa
(towards Pearl Harbor)
Waikiki
(towards Diamond Head)
Makai
(towards the sea)

A Bodima Book

13 Estates Drive, Orinda, California 94563

Introduction

A collection of flashbacks puts the present next to the past and raises some questions about both. But throughout there is the emergent question of the third comparative photograph, the missing future. Will decentralization shrink the towering skylines? Will architecture learn to live with climate again, instead of refrigerating it away? Will the driver evolve into a walker, a runner and a rider? How will solar energy and the planned economy change the look of a tropical city? Will the country infiltrate the town? This collection of comparative photographs shows the process of urban growth. At the same time it shows how rapidly the set of the movie we live in changes. There is no reason to believe it cannot rapidly change direction according to economic and social influences.

The transformation of Honolulu can thus be extrapolated to include factors more or less random, according to the way you look at them, like oil rationing and drought, or it can be projected according to the obvious growth trend in the area covered and the catch-up futures of the hinterland—will the Kona coast go high-rise? Will Maui become a suburban Oahu?

In some ways a balanced future will mean rediscovering the past, and the sheer speed of 20th century development invites nostalgia for the Waikiki of Victorian adventure, the organic horse-drawn environment, the quietness, the darkness.

But behind the picturesque was the grotesque: venereal disease, leprosy, plague, tuberculosis, extermination of sandalwood and whale, illiteracy, to name only a few afflictions. The native culture now embalmed for tourism was so despotic, sexist and superstitious that the female half of the Hawaiian race abandoned it at the first opportunity. As for the beloved horse, even if oil ran out tomorrow, drivers would use booze, sewage, sunshine, hot air, anything, to keep their cars running.

The set may never be picturesque again. The mess we live with is the result of so many conveniences. When students of urban affairs come to use comparative photography in the history of human habitat they will find that ugliness does not denote a bad living environment any more thanpicturesqueness indicates the garden of Eden. Many modern buildings are inside out. External appearances are sacrificed, even exaggerated, for a functional interior. Old buildings were the opposite. Absurd sacrifices were made to have a bank look like a Doric temple, or a barracks like a feudal fortress. We may settle for isolated sanctuaries, memory lanes where old urban sets are preserved.

American cities are poised near the end of the phase of central growth, towards the top of an exponential curve. Far from proceeding by lazy 'Hawaiian time' Hawaii is mutating into the future as fast as anywhere in the U.S.A. Suburban clones are sprouting everywhere, forcing legislators to question the ultimate carrying capacity of the state. The more it grows, the more it relies on imports factored by the big landowners. As it grows, the landowners' estates multiply in value. Even if the big estates accepted that limits on growth would immediately boost the value of development areas it is hard to see who could preside over such an apportionment in a market economy.

At the same time at points around the globe Hawaii is being touted as a tropical paradise draped with airbrushed hula girls. Tourists are invited to get away from it all in a city of hotels which by 1990 might house 200,000 (at double occupancy). Here the growth is doubly problematic. Tourism is the state's biggest industry, and a successful industry is axiomatically a growing one. Yet growth in this industry threatens the very product that is being sold: the environment. Inviting people over compounds the problem because so many want to come back to stay and 'me last' is an unconstitutional cry that confounds any politician who tries to exploit it. So, in the dilemma of the age, the unlimitable has to go on a diet. Some of the recipes have been pinned on the kitchen wall. A subway route is drawn up, a ferry system has been studied, surveys of historic buildings have been made, growth targets set,

decentralization adopted solar power publicized. But as yet the only decisive action is at Pearl Harbor where the U.S. navy, with military logic, has a fleet of free bicycles.

******

The comparative layouts jump about geographically to give a fresh, kaleidoscopic look at the process of change. They generally repeat a sequence of view, street scene, building.

References to history in the captions only briefly sketch the dramatic story of Honolulu, which is thoroughly covered in the extensive bibliography of Hawaiiana. The most accessible is Feher's **Pictorial History of Hawaii**. Few escape the pervasive influence of tourist mythology.

Grateful acknowledgment goes to Agnes Conrad and the staff at Hawaii state archives; Deborah Sullivan and the staff at the Bishop Museum; Frances Jackson at the University of Hawaii archives; the staff at Photoplant; Dr. Otto Degener; Joe Mullins; all the people who opened doors along the path of the old photographers; and not forgetting the intrepid photo-graphers themselves.

Roland Morgan
Mokuleia Beach
O'ahu

Index

BM denotes Bishop Museum, *UH* University of Hawaii, *SA* State Archives. All photographs by permission.

THEN Honolulu makai panorama 1885

Kou, Hawaii's only natural harbor, is the historic focus of Honolulu's growth dating back to its discovery by an English captain in 1792. A century later, when U.S. forces arrived during the Phillipines campaign, Pearl Harbor (out of picture, right) was developed and industry moved in that direction. Honolulu is a translation of Fair Haven, the short-lived English name for the harbor.

1

NOW Honolulu makai panorama

Building on a modern scale, including the drainage system, came with Hawaii's annexation into the U.S.A. during the Spanish-American war. Honolulu's cosmopolitan architecture today matches any comparable mainland city's. One peculiarity is the preponderance of offices downtown, most shopping having moved to the big Ala Moana center (out of picture left) in the early 1960's. The 1968 state capitol (left of center) stands out appropriately in this Punchbowl view.

THEN **King and Alakea Streets ewa makai 1883**
Billboards were banned in the islands in the 1920's. These early examples show Waikiki beach accommodation at $12 a week and Bull Durham, the first world-wide smoking campaign. The old telegraph pole (left) has been superseded by a tall new telephone pole for the service introduced to Honolulu in 1880.

3

NOW **King and Alakea Streets ewa makai**
This site is now occupied by the 1960's Finance Factors building, which features a unique array of adjustable louvered windows relying on electric light—a rejection of the climate.

THEN Fort and Queen Streets makai 1950

The powerful Hackfeld company had too many Hamburg connections for it to survive seizure during the 1914-18 European war, when it was renamed American Factors, later Amfac. The company's characterful 1901 stone pile boasted an ornate interior of marble, mosaic, wrought iron, fine wood and frescoes; certainly a unique Honolulu interior.

NOW **Fort and Queen Streets makai**
In 1968 American Factors tore down the
Hackfeld building to replace it with one of
their soaring 20-story foreshore towers.

THEN **Honolulu ewa panorama 1895**
The royal seat of power photographed a few years after the republican take-over. At left the Aliiolani Hale, at right the Iolani Palace. Office blocks and towers, shooting up in San Francisco, were yet to arrive at the crossroads of the Pacific.

7

NOW Honolulu ewa panorama

Honolulu's government center remains intact while the downtown core is transformed by a hodge-podge of office towers of varying degrees of obsolescence. In the foreground are the gardens of the Kawaiaha'o church where the picture is taken from. About half the land area in the picture is under occupation by motor vehicles, including the multi-storied parkade (mid-right), much larger than the trust company tower on its left.

THEN **Hotel Street at King waikiki 1898** (left)
The lei-makers (right) convey the intimate feel of the old harbor town shopping district. A boy could wander down the center of his street. Davey the photographer took some of the pictures in this book.

NOW **Hotel Street at King waikiki**
Development of the world's biggest shopping center two miles away at the gates of Waikiki's hotel stronghold froze this old focal point into the 1950's. Solar-powered overhead transit would bring a swift transformation.

THEN 250 South Hotel Street 1895

Spacious oval lanais were added to the front of the original Royal Hawaiian Hotel at the peak of its career as Honolulu's social center. Within a few years of this photo however, the nearby Young Hotel and the Moana and Seaside on Waikiki had taken most of the business and in 1917 the Royal Hawaiian was converted to a Young Men's Christian Association hostel.

Now **250 South Hotel**
The new YMCA building was
opened in 1928, its two front lanais
echoing the design of the old hotel.

12

THEN Looking west on
Nuuanu Pali pass 1885
This rugged road led from the busy port of Honolulu to the tranquil Hawaiian farmlands of Kaneohe. Here modern Hawaii's founder, King Kamehameha, defeated the warlord of O'ahu in 1795 using guns obtained from foreign traders.

NOW looking west on Nuuanu Pali pass

In the 1920's a smoother route was blasted between the peaks, but in the post-war boom this road became jammed and today's tunnels were drilled through the rock a hundred feet below.

THEN Kaneohe panorama north 1878

Primitive sugar mills like the one (center) at the foot of Lilipuna Road did not last long against the technology of cane kings like Claus Spreckels, who was at this time financing the Hawaiian government. Much of the area was still farmed by Hawaiians and Chinese. Fishponds (upper right) supplied the tables of Hawaiian chiefs. Typifying Hawaii's concentrated land ownership, sugar baron James Castle bought 340,000 acres here in 1917.

15

NOW **Kaneohe panorama north**
The arrival of suburban Honolulu has driven housing prices out of many people's reach. Isolated pockets of surviving farmers fight to keep their land.

THEN Ewa on King Street at Fort 1885

Honolulu's **haole's** built a harbor town just like on the mainland. Such was the quietness of downtown Honolulu in 1885 that just about all the folks knew they were having their picture taken. Night-time street lighting would not be introduced until the end of the decade.

17

NOW Ewa on King Street at Fort
Strangely devoid of shopping and, even more strangely, of a hotel, downtown Honolulu's one-way traffic arteries are no longer impressed by having their picture taken —a shutterbug could get run down, even if by a $20,000 sports model.

THEN **Fort Street at Pauahi waikiki makai 1890**
The catholic cathedral of Honolulu opened in 1843, after a decade of missionary opposition was overruled. Iron railings enclosed a spacious meeting yard.

19

NOW Fort Street at Pauahi waikiki makai
Modified extensively over the years, the cathedral gained weighty Doric pillars in 1929. With later removal of traffic from Fort Street the yard went open plan.

20

THEN Manoa Valley ewa panorama 1920
Hawaii Hall (center) was the first building on the Hawaii College 90-acre campus in 1912. This scene shows the college after it was named University of Hawaii, engineering quad at left, university farm in the foreground.

21

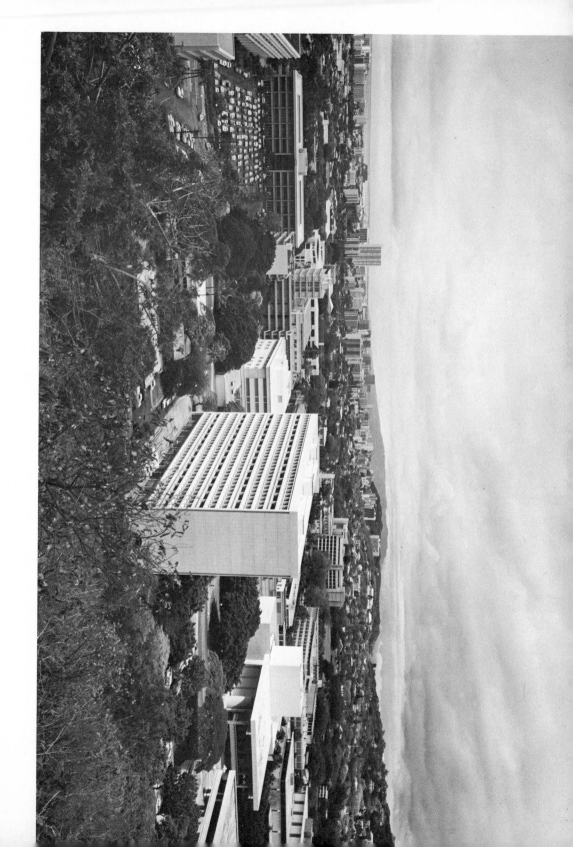

NOW **Manoa Valley ewa panorama**
Hale Manoa tower in the foreground demonstrates the dynamic growth of the university population. To its right is the Kennedy Theatre. Hawaii Hall is dwarfed amidst the 50 or so buildings added to campus. In the distance is the dense housing area towards Punchbowl.

THEN **Chinatown 1886**
The upper veranda frame building favored by the Chinese provided open air space for urban dwellers, most of them with businesses downstairs, and shade for the sidewalk beneath. Few examples of this once typical Hawaiian architecture survive.

23

Now Chinatown

While much of Hotel Street's commercial architecture dates back to the turn of the century its confusion of styles and the nature of local business suggest that even if Honolulu's planned rail transit relieves Hotel Street of its congestion, many buildings will be replaced. An urban renewal program also promises to raze most of the district.

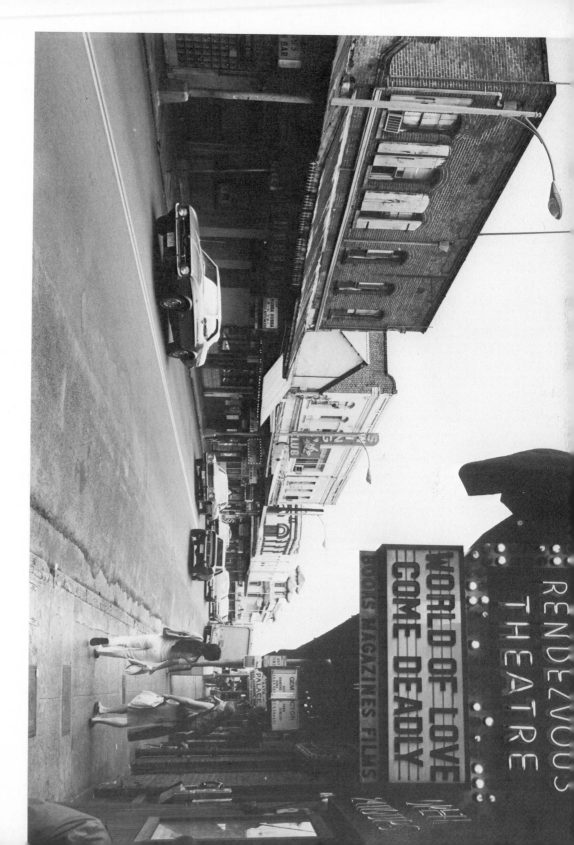

THEN 841 Bishop 1950 (left)
The Theo. H. Davies building was built in 1919 for one of Hawaii's 'big five' trading companies, from an otherwise forgotten downtown plan drawn up by its architect. A striking Italian Renaissance design made entirely from reinforced concrete and cut stone, the building doubled as offices and warehouse, incorporating loading bays at the rear.

NOW 841 Bishop
Tragically the warehousing function of the Davis building became incompatible with downtown Honolulu in the 1970's and the high-rise Davies Pacific Center was built in its place. Imaginative street level design, however, gave the city a new space which made up for the architectural loss.

THEN mauka panorama from judiciary building 1891 (left)
At right is the barracks of the royal guard. At center is Iolani Palace, occupied by the ill-fated Queen Liliuokalani. At left behind the palace is the royal private quarters, beyond it in the distance are St. Andrew's Cathedral and the Royal Hawaiian Hotel. Railings had been substituted for the high palace walls by a jittery legislature in 1890. Coats of arms on the gates show the monarchy still intact.

NOW mauka panorama from judiciary building
The 1968 legislature occupies the site of the barracks which in turn occupy the site of the royal bungalow. After serving as the republican executive building for 75 years the restored palace was opened to the public exactly a century after its founding.

28

T HEN Fort Street at Hotel makai 1898
Honolulu's main shopping street in the heyday of the modern city. Most of the conveniences, few of the blights. Windows were shuttered in case of riots in the streets. The electric arc lamp (bottom right) was on a pulley for daily replacement of the arc.

29

NOW **Fort Street at Hotel makai**
The aging commercial structures of Fort Street,
overshadowed by business towers, invite redevelopment.

THEN Kapiolani Park 1900

No North American town in the horse-drawn age could imagine life without somewhere to race the steeds and place some bets on the results. The long-forgotten structures of the Kapiolani Park race track looked ghostly without their crowds.

31

NOW Kapiolani Park

Where gaitered puritans and barefoot immigrants once mingled for a horse race their descendants gather at 7 a.m. on a Sunday morning for a bracing run. Diamond Head looms unmoved.

THEN **Honolulu waikiki panorama 1887**
The old New England missionary church of 1842, Kawaiaha'o, became the shrine of Hawaiian royalty. King Lunalilo had his tomb built by the church door in 1874. Beyond stretch the swamps of Ala Moana, Kewalo Basin and Ala Wai, Diamond Head swathed in haze.

33

NOW **Honolulu waikiki panorama**
The architecturally undistinguished territorial building was built in 1926 to house government offices. It is shown here under restoration. Diamond Head is lost behind a wall of towers at Waikiki.

34

THEN Fort Street mauka view 1859

A new landmark on Fort Street was the Congregational church (spire, center) built by the missionaries for Honolulu's **haole** population in 1852. The Bartlett Saloon (bottom left) would have been out of bounds for Hawaiian natives. At far left are the offices of pioneer photographer J.L. Chase, who took the picture.

35

NOW Fort street mauka view
After a period of intense traffic congestion, some of the greenery has returned to Fort Street. The commercial buildings date back to the turn of the century, disguised by numerous facelifts. Most shopping has moved away from old Honolulu to new shopping centers.

THEN 140 South King Street 1925

The Bank of Hawaii moved from its Merchant Street premises in the 1920's to a building in the Mediterranean style favored by members of the 'big five' trading companies in the same era, giving downtown Honolulu a period of pleasing architectural consistency in tune with the climate.

NOW 140 South King Street

By the 1960's the high-rise opportunities were too tempting and the bank moved across King Street to the Castle and Cooke financial plaza. The bank building was demolished and replaced by the sheer International-style tower of the Bishop Trust, handsomely sheathed in sepia-tinted reflecting glass.

THEN Waikiki Beach 1880

The Occidental Hotel (left) was owned by a steamship line. The royal villa was a few yards further down the beach. A sober suit, beard and hat were the **haole** uniform.

NOW Waikiki Beach (right)

Jet planes bring millions of sun-seekers to Waikiki every year and the set is transformed, but the underlying pattern remains the same, with many of the hotels interlinked by ownership with their carriers. **Haole's** stripped to loin cloths in the 1920's in search of the tan made fashionable by the jazz age.

THEN Hobron Lane at Ala Moana *makai* **1944**
It's not far back in time to a Waikiki of sandy lanes, ramshackle beach huts and happy-go-lucky parking.

41

NOW Hobron Lane at Ala Moana makai

Honolulu's big yacht marina was built at the foot of Hobron Lane soon after installation of Ala Moana boulevard in 1954. Accommodation racks servicing jet age tourists now crowd the beach and cars stop on the streets only in the small hours.

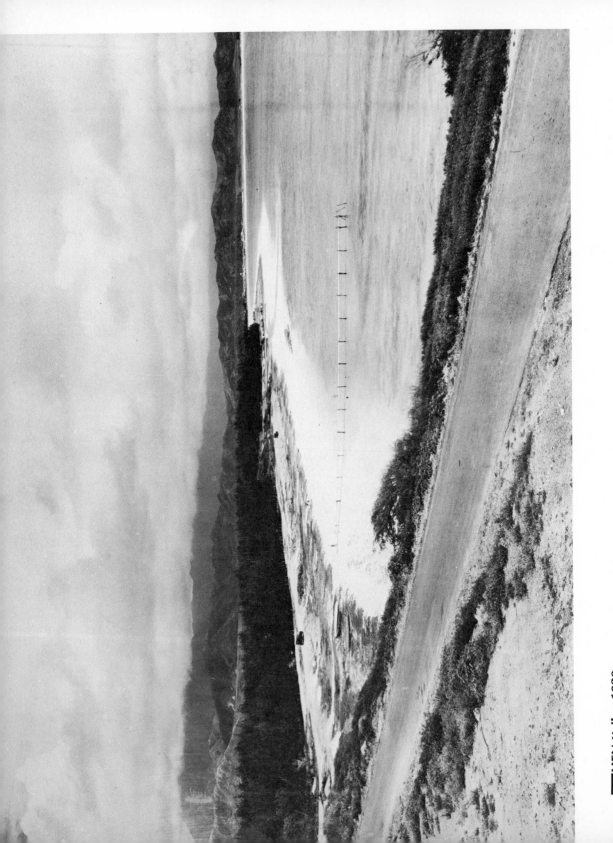

THEN Kailua 1920

A former captial of O'ahu, Kailua once held the bulk of the island's Hawaiian population. They lived among cocoanut groves and fishponds which have since turned into inland swamps. By 1920 a metalled coast road had been installed and Honolulu's suburbs were moving in.

N OW Kailua

Kailua is now a model grid suburb, connected to Honolulu by two freeways through the mountains.

THEN **Honolulu waterfront 1895**
Trade was concentrated within three blocks either side of Fort Street, light offshore schooners mooring against international clippers willy-nilly. Giant wooden vessels (right) were being replaced by ships with iron hulls.

45